The Little Bluebird of Happiness

By C. Everett

Copyright © 2017 C. Everett

All rights reserved.

ISBN:
ISBN-13: 978-0-9994624-3-0

DEDICATION

To Aunt Poci, who gave me the little (glass) bluebird of happiness
And to Little Tot (aka Flash) who was one

The bluebird has been known in many cultures over the world, as a symbol of happiness, hope, joy and renewal.

And when he sings to you
Though you're deep in blue
You will see a ray of light creep through
And so remember this, life is no abyss
Somewhere there's a bluebird of happiness

From "Bluebird of Happiness" Song written by
Sandar Harmati and Edward Heyman
1934

ACKNOWLEDGMENTS

Stock Photos provided by
Dreamstime

In a very big forest, far, far away, there was a little bluebird who loved to sing. He sang because it made him happy, and because it made those around him happy.

When he arose he sang a good day to the fading moon, he sang a bright hello to the rising sun and he sang his thank you to the new morning. During the day he sang to the other birds and to the forest, and at night he sang sweetly to the stars.

The little bluebird kept singing as he grew, and if he was feeling a little sad or bad, he would remember to sing. His songs were a beautiful and magical sound, and the more he sang the happier he became, and the happier he became the more he sang.

The other birds taught the little bluebird their songs and he taught them his. The forest echoed with their chirps and melodies, and the creatures of the forest would stop and admire the chorus.

One day, though, there was a terrible storm. The wind blew so hard that it carried the little bluebird far away to the other side of the forest, and though he tried, he could not find his way back home.

The forest here seemed darker and the air heavier, and the birds he met on this side of the forest were very different from the birds he had known at home. These birds were always grouchy and complaining about some thing or another!

It seemed to the little bluebird that the birds in this part of the forest always found a reason to not be happy. So, the little bluebird tried talking to them to cheer them up, but that just seemed to make them even grouchier!

He brought them presents, but they still were unhappy. The birds said they might be happier if the worms were fatter, or if it rained, or didn't rain, or if it was hotter or colder, but they were determined to be unhappy and didn't want his presents.

The little bluebird could not make worms fatter, so he did what he did best and sang to the birds, but they then complained that happy singing only reminded them of how unhappy they were.

The little bluebird did not know what else to do, and soon became unhappy himself. His light dimmed, and he began walking with his head drooping and his feet shuffling, like the other birds, and started complaining about every little thing.

There seemed to be a cloud over the little bluebirds' head and he wondered why he ever bothered being happy to begin with. His unhappiness pleased the other birds, because if they were unhappy, then they wanted everyone else to be unhappy as well.

One night the little bluebird couldn't sleep and flew here and there until he saw a wise owl watching him.

"Whoo, whoo," said the owl, "I see an unhappy bluebird!"

The little bluebird told his story of how he lost his happiness, feeling sorry for himself and sure the owl would feel sorry for him too, but to his surprise the owl chuckled merrily.

"True happiness," he smiled "comes from choosing to be happy no matter where you are or who you are with!"

"If you wait for the worms to get fatter," he continued, "or the sun to shine, or the rain to flow, then you will only ever find little bits of happiness that won't last. Real happiness must come from within, and once you knew that!"

The owl put on his glasses and pointed north. "Now, if you really want to go home, just fly that way. Good luck, little bluebird!"

The little bluebird returned to his nest. As the sun rose he began to sing, and he sang until he felt the happiness return inside of him. Some of the other birds heard him and secretly smiled at the beauty of his song, while others frowned, but the bluebird wished them all the chance to find their own happiness, and then, when he was ready, he flew north.

Now the little bluebird remembered that with the happiness that comes from within, that even if at times he felt bad or sad, those feelings would never last very long. So with a lighter heart he flew all day and all night, until he didn't think he could fly much further, but he gathered his strength and kept going with the thought that he would soon be home.

In the morning he came upon other birds that he recognized and knew that he was finally home. He greeted the other birds with a grateful heart and then finally rested from his adventure.

The next morning, before the dawn, a little bluebird sang. He sang a good day to the fading moon, he sang a bright hello to the rising sun, he sang his thank you to the new morning, and he vowed he would never again hide his light or lose his joy.

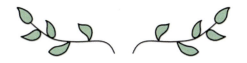

In a very big forest, far, far away, a little bluebird lost his way and then found his way back home. He loved to sing, and creatures from all over the forest came to hear the little bird sing his happy songs. He became legendary throughout the forest, and would forever more be known as "The Little Bluebird of Happiness".

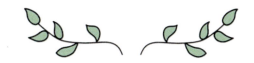

C. Everett

ABOUT THE AUTHOR

C. Everett grew up with a fondness and respect for all creatures and what they have to teach us, including the beautiful birds that give us their songs in the morning. She hopes you enjoy these stories and wishes you all your own Bluebird of Happiness!

Made in the USA
Las Vegas, NV
13 December 2022